D1776024

IN LOVE
IS AN EXPENSIVE
PLACE
TO DIE

IN LOVE IS AN EXPENSIVE PLACE TO DIE

POEMS BY JOHN LAWS

PAUL HAMLYN

SYDNEY
LONDON
NEW YORK
TORONTO

PUBLISHED BY PAUL HAMLYN PTY. LTD.
176 SOUTH CREEK ROAD, DEE WHY WEST
N.S.W. 2099 FIRST PUBLISHED 1971
REPRINTED 1974
COPYRIGHT PAUL HAMLYN PTY. LTD. 1971

PRODUCED IN AUSTRALIA BY THE PUBLISHER
TYPESET IN AUSTRALIA BY PHOTOTYPE-SALES
PRINTED IN HONG KONG

NATIONAL LIBRARY OF AUSTRALIA REGISTRY NO. ISBN 0 600 070379

CONTENTS

The day you came into my life,
the way you came into my life.
You stood.
And you gave my lonely heart
a brand new lease of love.
A love we didn't know we needed.
And yet our empty hearts just pleaded,
beating strong.
Though forbidden in our mind,
that made our love a special kind.
But that kind of love isn't easy.
And I wish that life was as easy,
as to hold you, and to love you.
And I always will in my mind,
'cause our love's that special kind.
One day I'll walk right out of your life,
the way your love came into my life.
'Cause we know,
that the world won't let us last,
but our futures hold our past.

one

I just turned the hot water on to wash a glass for
another drink
so now I'll just sit here and wait for the hot
water service to turn itself on and bubble.
The trouble
with me in comparison with the HWS is when you
take something out of me I need a drink,
to think,
and turn me on.
Take something out of the HWS and it will just
turn itself on and bubble,
no trouble.
Actually I have an HWS problem,
only my HWS doesn't mean hot water service
it means husband and wife separation.
I just wish I had the inclination
to turn me on and bubble again,
but my heart
can't start
to replace a love gone down the drain.
That's one love that ended up in the sewer of life
I guess
and all because of an HWS.

two

8

three

Let's buy an orange car with a slit in the roof.
I want the slit in the roof because
that just might let some sun in.
And that sun's pretty powerful and
that just might let some fun in too.
Apart from that, with a slit in the roof
of your orange car
you would find it much easier to commune
with nature,
and if the sun's on your face
it won't seem so bad when you grate your gears.
Apart from that a bird might fly in.
Somebody once said a bird in the car
is worth a slit in the roof.

four

I decided when I left you that I would only allow my
heart the luxury of crying once a year,
and for the remaining months every thought of you
would completely disappear.
The thought of your small body thudding heavily
onto the sand under the weight of mine,
neither of us caring who cared, or shared, the
knowledge that we were in love at the time.
The thought of having only $200 in the whole world
and spending it in two weeks
trying to impress you without making a slip,
pretending to have something when I had nothing and
I didn't even know how to tip the waiter.
You knew but you didn't care,
and it wasn't until tonight I remembered being there.
I remember people saying I wasn't right for you,
and your mother implored you, I'll bet
to forget me—
but you didn't care because you knew I adored you.
I'll also forget the thought of a hot day in a car,
a hundred degree drive
when hot, or not, love made me stand on the brakes
and hold you.

That was when love was alive.
The thought of boating – trying to row and smoke
a pipe, which must have looked pretty funny –
and the two of us in our first car which we both washed
and said we'd have to keep at least a year
because we didn't have any money.
The thoughts of poetry I wrote for our little boy
to show you how much I loved the child.
The way I used to boast about him driving the car
at nine months while you just sat and smiled.
Damn the thoughts.
I only think them once a year,
why should I want to remember.
All these thoughts and an occasional tear
seem to last from January to December.

five

You must admit it's quite a status symbol
to own your own private world.
I do
I do what I like in my own world.
I even love a little privately.

This I write for the social upstart who wants
to tear a man apart
because he dares to speak his mind to that
very special kind of fake
Who goes through life no give all take.
That's sad.
Your daddy bought you this and that,
a poodle dog, a Siamese cat,
vintage wine, fillet steak,
but he couldn't buy you heartbreak.

six

That's bad.
It may take a lot of years before you ever
cry real tears,
tears that one day go to make a person live
for another's sake.
I'm glad.
I know that it's tougher to suffer.
So all those words that to me you have spoken,
won't break my heart 'cause it's already broken.
You're too late . . .
for anything.

seven

When I sit with a pen in my hand,
I sometimes write your name –
it makes me feel close to you.
I often write a card but it's
never quite the same –
as when I sent a rose to you.
But now when I write it,
it isn't quite as plain –
the ink no longer flows for you.
Why does love dry up like a pen
that's written too many names
or a man who's known too many shames.
No one really knows but you.

Temporary is the breath you take
when your body hits cold water.
Temporary is a blink.
Temporary is permanence only shorter.
Temporary is whatever you think.
Temporary is whatever you think.
Temporary is a feeling that runs through your skin –
Temporarily to a touch.
Temporary is a wish when emotions begin.
Temporary is really not much.
Temporary is the feeling of style
when the sheets are made of silk.
Temporary makes no sense.
Temporary is a room service glass of milk.
Temporary is your defence.
Temporary is the excuse you make
when you think you are in too deep.
Temporary is kissing.
Temporary defines the sleep I'm missing
Temporarily if you're clever.
Temporary for you I'm prepared to be –
Temporarily forever.

eight

I really think the greatest thought destroyer in
the world is the telephone.
It's rather like mankind's immunisation
against Cupid.
Now that might sound a little stupid,
but how many times have you sat with your mind
like a bucket of mud
because something soils your love like a snail
soils a rosebud.
Then through your mud mind comes the answer,
talk to her.
So you walk about in your room

nine

trying to think of something to talk about
in the gloom of your mind.
You thread all the thoughts together as carefully
as an old lady threads a needle to do some tapestry,
probably trying to find escape from
her own muddy mind.
Words are pretty hard to find
when you want to be tender and kind.
But like a school kid writing an essay,
you carefully plan what you're going to say.
I really should be firm and gentle,
God I'll go mental if I can't find a way to say
I love you.

If you're like me you just sit there with your
mud bucket mind going round and round
like You and Me in a fish tank,
and you thank God you don't argue every day.
You finally talked yourself into believing
you really cared,
you finish the speech you carefully prepared,
partly to deceive her.
Then all alone
you just sit there and grab the phone,
but as soon as she lifts the receiver
it's all gone,
every carefully-contrived word, every thought,
every inflection.
Gone, flown with its tail between its legs
in the opposite direction,
like a disobedient dog.
All you want to do is tell
Alexander Graham Bell
to go to hell.
Well, I wish he had.
It's bad to hide behind a phone like
a small boy behind his mother's skirt,
just because you think your pride might be hurt.

Be a man . . . there's no disgrace . . .
in being sorry face to face.

ten

How the hell can they call it a motel suite when
it's anything but.
It may be complete and neat and discreet –
If you have a love that hides behind deceit.
But at the moment mine doesn't –
so to me it's just a box of loneliness with a john.

I only hope, my little boy,
that we can share those special feelings given by
somebody big-feelings that I share as a man.
That would really be some toy.
If I could give you the ability to feel humility
just by looking at something nature created
as part of nature's appreciation plan.
I want you to love not only as a man but
as a sensitive human being, alive seeing,
and wondering how many people go through life
blundering over material things that anyone can buy.

eleven

Try to find a man who can be content looking
at cold water shining over coloured stones
and you'll find a man who's never alone.
Try to be that man.
Be a supporter of nature's appreciation plan.
Look, feel and love.
Look at clouds, feel the wind and love love.
Keep the wonder of a little boy even when
you're fully grown,
and you keep all those special feelings
not many men have known.

Forget about that day last week when things
were not so bad.
Or smile a thought about that love you
nearly almost had.
Forget about the fire you felt before
you slapped his face.
And how you self-indulged next day –
like a baby in disgrace.
Forget about most everything–forget to wonder why.
'Cause if you forget to forget about –
you'll forget about not to cry.
Forget about the tear you shed because
you thought you should.
And how good you felt when you shed it –
'cause you never thought you could.
Forget about that horror film
that really wasn't horrid.
Forget about that little line on the
right side of your forehead.
Forget about a love you left early one December.
Forget about it if you can–but don't forget
that I remember

twelve

thirteen

What a drag it is when you've read about the sun,
and a clap of thunder
brings you to your senses, when you were under
the impression that looking at the words
would simply make it happen.
Well, the best thing to do is to read another line
concentrate . . . and then see if the sun will shine.
But remember, if the clouds are still
grey and dirty when you look,
you can always read another book.

fourteen

Loneliness is nothing.
Nothing is me when I am lonely.
You are everything.
Everything is me when I'm with you.
Absence is proof.
Proof is what I get when I am lonely.
So loneliness is necessary.
Necessary is what you become when I'm lonely.
Loneliness is something.

fifteen

If a man was to tell another man the way men do
that he was having trouble loving
because of a small boy,
the other man would suggest instant psychiatry,
with definite finality,
and talk with pompous piety
of latent homosexuality.
That is a problem.
To want to love the way men do and be capable of
treating a woman like a toy,
to be ready and waiting and filled with passion
uninhibited without disgrace,
to love in more ways than the accepted fashion,
then have desire drowned by a small boy's face.
You wouldn't think that sort of power
could be within a child,
to make a man turn away from some erotic joy,
to change a man from passion to something
kind and mild.
But I'm not ashamed of my small boy thoughts,
that small boy is my child.

sixteen

Me and You (which is bad grammar)
spent their lives going round and round
and everybody said-what a tragic existence.
And so did I, until I found
if you go round and round
you get back to where you've been.
And I've never seen a man who at sometime
or other didn't have the wish to go back.
There's only one problem –
Me and You are fish.
Well, at least we can wish.

seventeen

Why can't we pick lovers,
just like we pick roses.
Pick a rose and it never really knows us as we are.
A rose doesn't ask questions.
It doesn't ask why we have sad eyes,
or why we like to be alone.
It never tries to psychoanalyse
the whys and wherefores of apparent misery.
A rose never complains out loud.
it just smells sweet.
At least temporarily.
Then the petals fall like a broken heart.
Love and a rose aren't very far apart-are they.

eighteen

You came to me too quickly, like tomorrow.
Your nearness is as real as yesterday.
The touch of you is as sensitive as sorrow.
And forever is quietly how you'll stay.

nineteen

Why the hell would I write poetry.
Probably because I'm trying to find
another way to say I've loved.
God how I've loved.
What a lousy feeling to love that much
and not have the guts to say so.
I've held those words inside and nearly
choked on them
because I thought my love might make you dirty.
So rather than take the risk of saying
something you might scorn,
I've fought the other way like a wounded animal.
Then you went away.
Now you're not here I can say
I love you.
One day you may look at this book
and remember you loved too –
at least I think you did.

The trouble with average hairspray
is no one has average hair.
And the trouble with the average problem is the
average person doesn't care.
The trouble with my heart is it never
had an average affair.
But what about the average man who goes home
on the train and reads about the war
every day, winter and summer.
Same train, same war, same wife,
being aware of all the strife in the world
but not really caring because

twenty

he never had any in his own life.
The trouble with the average train ride is nobody
sees the average train,
and the trouble with the average winter is nobody
feels the average rain.
The people reading the average paper should stop
and use their average brain –
if everything was average there
would be nothing to compare,
ride the train,
read the paper,
but do without something you love,
and you'll soon know how much you loved it
when it was there.

The trouble with the average tear is that
it comes from an average eye.
You look at the average bird and expect
the average thing to fly
You go and buy your average hairspray
and you never wonder why.
Well, all the average people would really much prefer
to be like the people who aren't average
but really wish they were.
It doesn't hurt so much.

twenty-one

Let's go somewhere else –
here is too near.
Somewhere else is far away.

I would love to hate you because you proved to me
that I have the ability to love.
I used to love loving, and one of my favourite words
was forever because I believed it.
I used to love laughing, and one of my
favourite words was happiness
because I believed that too.
But now forever is fear because it means
a lifetime without you

twenty-two

and laughter is a memory, just one of many
that I have about you.
You taught me to love, now you have taught me not to,
but you haven't forgotten to forget
that I have got to
because if I can't love I can't live –
and love is the best thing that a man has to give.
Because I gave my love to you because I really cared,
I can't give love to anyone now.
I am scared . . . scared . . . scared.

twenty-three

I remember sitting myself for long periods under
a tree watching the leaves fall.
If I was a good poet I would have said
long, lonely periods,
but really they weren't lonely at all –
because you were always there with me.
And as each leaf would float to the ground, like
a water-logged stick in a still pond,
I'd think about love.
Our love was once like a healthy tree that stretched
its arms out like a new baby who stretches
and doesn't know why.
I always thought of that as a kind of sapling love,
like a little tree who's proud and wants to push
its way through to the sky.
That's just how it was with us.
But as our little tree got older, the branches
got brittle, and we had all sorts of intruders.
Sometimes a butcher bird, sometimes a dove,
and then slowly –
because probably our tree cared, more about growing
than knowing –
we found the intruders were more than we could take.

And right in the sunshine of our lives, when we should
have been strong and proud,
the tree became unsure of itself and
occasionally it would shake,
and when it did each leaf that fell
became a dream or a hope.
And finally one day, I saw my own heart
falling from above.
But have you ever watched a leaf fall,
fragile and small, from a tall tree –
every now and then a breath of air catches it
and it goes up again –
well, that's how it is with me.
Now my life is like a tired tree living on
the moisture of a covered up tear,
hoping that occasionally a little breeze of love would
lift my heart
to where it was when you were near.
But no love is that strong.
Just the same as no man's heart deserves a living death,
so please try and love me,
but take a deep breath.

twenty-four

Don't be nice to her it could turn to love.
Heavens above, that would never do.
You had better systematically
and emphatically verbally attack her
so she'll think about you the way others do.
Then if she does cling
it's only because she means it.

twenty-five

The ad man told me I should think pink.
The newspaper said think about crime.
My heart said think about someone else –
but I couldn't think of anything at the time.
The Government said think about paying your tax.
The Preacher said God was divine.
My heart said think about thinking of you –
but I couldn't think of anything at the time.
What's the point in thinking, or linking all
my thoughts together.
The only thing I really think is I'll think
of you forever.
Think about kindness,
think about you,
think about love in its prime.
I wanted to think of the things that I think,
but I couldn't think of anything at the time.

I remember one occasion
one 86 proof invasion
of my mind.
I thought booze was consolation
but it's simply irrigation
of a kind.
I am depressed, the world hates me.
I will just slip out and have a booze or two
and do a test on how the public rates me.
Make a friend or lose a few.
You know there is one thing about booze
that is funny,
it has a hidden alcoholic trick.
All I can ever seem to lose is money,
and all I make is me–sick.
Sometimes I just sit and think
and irrigate my sorrows with a drink or two,
while I hold my tears back blinking,
thinking of the look of you.
And in the midst of all the headache drinking
and the sour mash 86 proof thinking,
with every drink I drink,
and every thought I think,
there are 86 proof heartache thoughts of you.

twenty·six

I often sit and wonder whether
even if I hadn't strayed we would still
have been together,
loving the way we did when two of us on a tram gave
the tram a brand new social standing in our eyes.
We thought of the evening star as our own special
love jewel and we told each other loving lies.
I called you little one, and promised I would
love you forever, and I wanted to.
But age didn't make me very clever,
it only made me think I was.

twenty-seven

I can never have again that special kind of
hand-in-hand love that only
comes the first time.
I remember deplorable attempts to write
poetry for you because I always thought
that love belonged in rhyme.
I doubt if I could stand that sort of love again
because I could only compare it with that special love.
That love, according to song-writers and poets,
has withered and died.
It's not dead, but if it was,
it would be you who had killed it with pride.

Everybody should learn to like trains
'cause life is sort of like a long rail journey
full of little sidings, some good, some bad.
Any man who ever had an ounce of commonsense,
or used his will has told himself to get up and move on
'cause they just milk the cow that
stands still.
Trains can be held up at a siding for 20 or 30 minutes.
Could be a beautiful little glen,
could be an ugly work camp.

twenty-eight

Whatever it is, it's not the end of the journey.
Sometimes when you're young you think it is.
Even though it's not too bad,
you expected something better,
like when you were a kid on Christmas morning,
looking for that special present
you were sure you would get.
Then you had to fight back the tears
'cause it wasn't what you thought it was.
Marriage is only a siding,
and never blame a woman for that, it's not her fault.
Blame God.

Don't get out the photographs,
they'll only make you cry.
Don't get out the letters,
or you'll sit and wonder why.
Wonder why and how and when and where
that love went to.
And it's going to blow your ego,
'cause she made it without you.
Don't get out that record,
'cause you'll only sit and play it.
Don't think about that poetry,
or you'll think of how she'd say it.
How she'd say, how she'd walk, and even how she'd do.
But it's going to knock your pride around,
'cause she made it without you.

twenty-nine

Don't drive past the house you had,
you'll look the other way.
Don't go in that coffee shop,
you went with her one day.
Don't go here, don't go there,
don't go anywhere she knew.
And it's going to break your heart some more
'cause she's been there without you.
Put away your memories, put away your life.
Put away a little girl who used to be your wife.
Put away this, put away that,
put away things that were.
But you can't put away that one simple fact,
you can't make it without her.

Whatever happened to the day when we had our
own private world when it didn't matter.
We'd go to a party and just see each other,
both being bored by stupid chatter.
All we wanted to do was get away so we could
devote our time entirely to each other,
and not have to worry about false smiles and
Would you care for another?

Whatever happened to the day when neither of us
could have cared for another human being,
and seeing each other was the most important thing
in the world–nothing else mattered a bit.
It didn't matter whether we were sitting in a movie
looking at a bald-headed man dance,
or waiting to meet each other
on the corner of King and Pitt.
Every song in every movie became our song,
and every street corner became deserted
when you came along.
Whatever happened to the days before the nights
When we were under the same roof
but in separate rooms,
and I used to tap the wall hoping that you,
But nobody else, would hear so you might come in
and we could be near, again.
That was all that counted to me.
If you were near I was safe, protected.
Who would have suspected
that there could be a flaw in a love like that.
Whatever happened to the day I just found myself
crying because I just missed you,
And I'd just lie and think about the last time
I kissed you
in front of about 40 people at an airport
in the middle of nowhere.

Whatever happened to the day when love was
so beautiful, clouds were bright,
everything in life was right.
Now I sit and look at night
and sometimes I softly say,
perhaps sometime you'll wonder
whatever happened to the day.

thirty

thirty-one

From where I sit I hear voices
coming from faces I never see.
Just voices talking at me.
I listen and wonder what the faces
and the people behind them are like.
Wondering why they were the ones who
wanted to strike up a conversation.
Lonely loveless people with a wasted word
trying to recapture the times
they heard a word of love.
I'll give it.

thirty-two

I am fascinated that people know how to run my life
and even get the odd pound off my wife.
But the part that is really hell, you see,
is that they tell everybody and won't tell me.
They say I am irresponsible, bad,
and for my poor little child it must be very sad.
But he seems quite happy with his bad old pa
out in the boat and out in the car,
and his mind's just beautiful –
there's not a wrinkle in his brow –
and he is not damning other people,
because he doesn't know how.
I just wish they would let he and me be
because I need him and he needs me.
Perhaps I need their help, it may well be,
but they just tell their friends but never tell me.

thirty-three

Does anybody have a tissue,
I think my heart's caught a chill.
I fell asleep in the draught of love
and a frozen heart could kill.
Does anybody have a tissue.
I could also dry my eye.
I could spread it wide and could hide this face
so the world won't see me cry.
Does anybody have a tissue to wipe
a small boy's tears and also wipe away
a love he thought would last for years.
Does anybody have a tissue to wipe
the whole world's eyes.

Why is it you say:
I'm going to speak slowly and clearly because
I want you to understand every word I say.
Does that indicate to me that you couldn't care less
whether I hear or not
when you talk the other way,
which you generally do.
Why do you talk at all if you don't want me to hear
when you spit words out like a gun with a twisted barrel,
telling me I ruined your day.
What a waste of woman auditioning to one man.
It sounds like reading from an uncensored
Arthur Miller play,
get out go away.
I generally do,
if not physically, because I'm pretty hard to budge.
Every time you spit words
you give love a gentle nudge.
Love's such a little word,
what did it ever do to hurt you.
So next time you're speaking slowly and clearly
so I can hear every word,
say something pleasant.
That way speed and clarity are immaterial,
from the first to the last each word will be heard.
That's generally true.

thirty-four

thirty-five

I heard you talk to a woman today,
you had no right to say what you did.
Who in the world are you trying to kid.
I said what I said, I did what I did,
and I'll say it today or tomorrow or any other day.
Even if you don't agree with the things that I say
or the prayer that I pray, or the way that I pray it
never deny me the right to say it.
My right is my prize.
Who are you to be so critical?
Have you ever thought that in my eyes
you have no right to be analytical,
criticise, analyse, ostracise,
But never fight the fact
that all men have a right
no matter what your eyes are seeing
to be a normal human being.

thirty-six

Was it Monday morning's wishful thought,
or Monday evening's dream,
or Tuesday's friend so carefully bought,
for Tuesday's night-time scheme.
Or Wednesday morning's hearty meal,
or Wednesday's night-time hunger,
or Thursday's hour trying to steal,
a Thursday night much younger.
Was it Friday morning's gladness,
that Friday's night closed the week,
to bring on Saturday's sadness,
and a Saturday lover to seek.
Or Sunday morning's empty hours,
or Sunday evening's blue,
that made me cry for a love once ours,
an everyday love with no you.

thirty-seven

You're quite right –
it should all stop.
But can it.
Our love will keep rising to the top
like cream on a glass of milk,
and even if the milk turns sour
our love won't.
God knows both cream and love are luxuries.
So why waste them on somebody else's glass of life.

thirty-eight

There are so many things that I want to do,
but I just run out of drive.
There are so many things to share with you,
yet I wonder why I'm alive.
My world's mine and yours is yours,
and I really don't want to change it.
But I think that love is the primary cause,
why I'd like to re-arrange it.
There's so much love I could give to you,
I just want that you should know it.
There are so many reasons to live for you,
I just wish that I could show it.
My world's mine and yours is yours,
and I know that yours is free.
But I don't want to live in this world of mine,
if I must live here as me.

WE ARE ALL BORN EQUAL . I just
happen to be a little bit more
equal,

THE PEOPLE WHOSE ATTENTION YOU SHOU
TRY TO HOLD IS THE ATTENTION
OF THOSE WHO WANT TO LISTEN.

THERE IS NO ONE BETTER THAN ME AND I'M
NO BETTER THAN ANYONE ELSE. A.J.Fayr